Did You

THE CINQ

A MISCELLANY

Compiled by Julia Skinner

With particular reference to the work of Paul Harris, Alan Kay,
Rex Marchant and Barrie Wootton

THE FRANCIS FRITH COLLECTION

www.francisfrith.com

First published in the United Kingdom in 2012 by The Francis Frith Collection®

This edition published exclusively for Bradwell Books in 2012
For trade enquiries see: www.bradwellbooks.com or tel: 0800 834 920
ISBN 978-1-84589-694-2

British Library Cataloguing in Publication Data

Did You Know? The Cinque Ports - A Miscellany
Compiled by Julia Skinner
With particular reference to the work of Paul Harris, Alan Kay, Rex Marchant and Barrie Wootton

The Francis Frith Collection
Oakley Business Park,
Wylye Road, Dinton,
Wiltshire SP3 5EU
Tel: +44 (0) 1722 716 376
Email: info@francisfrith.co.uk

www.francisfrith.com

Printed and bound in Malaysia
Contains material sourced from responsibly managed forests

Front Cover: **RAMSGATE, THE HARBOUR CROSSWALL 1907** 58287p
Frontispiece: **DOVER, THE PROMENADE 1908** 60393
Contents: **FOLKESTONE, THE HARBOUR 1912** 65005

The colour-tinting is for illustrative purposes only, and is not intended to be historically accurate

CONTENTS

2   Introduction

8   The Cinque Ports Miscellany

46 Sporting Cinque Ports

47 Haunted Cinque Ports

48 Quiz Questions

50 Recipes

52 Quiz Answers

54 Francis Frith - Pioneer Victorian
    Photographer

INTRODUCTION

The Confederation of the Cinque Ports was a group of medieval ports, all but one in Kent and East Sussex, which in return for considerable rights and privileges provided the monarch with vessels and mariners for ship service, thus forming an important naval force of the Middle Ages. As its name suggests, there were originally five ports in the Confederation (although 'Cinque' is pronounced 'sink', not 'sank', as in the French word 'cinq' for five), but many other places were linked with it over the centuries, as corporate or non-corporate members. At least 23 towns are known to have been connected with the Confederation at its height, but there may actually have been as many as 42.

Moving west to east along the south-eastern coast, the original five 'Head Ports' of the Confederation were Hastings, New Romney, Hythe, Dover and Sandwich. After originally being 'limbs' of Hastings to help that port with its ship service obligations, Rye and Winchelsea became the sixth and seventh 'Head Ports' in the 14th century, with the title of 'The Two Ancient Towns'. These places all had harbours in the medieval period and fishing fleets manned by skilful crews that could be turned into fighting ships if and when necessary. However, most of these places are no longer important ports – their harbours silted up over the centuries, and in some cases the shoreline has receded so far away that they are now inland settlements some distance from the sea.

The Confederation of the Cinque Ports probably dates back to the reign of the Anglo-Saxon King Edward the Confessor (1042-1066), who traded rights and privileges with the original five Head Ports in return for them providing ships and men to help repel raiders attacking his kingdom, and to defend and maintain the transportation links across the English Channel to the Continent. Following his victory over King Edward's successor, King Harold, at the Battle of Hastings of 1066 and the subsequent Norman Conquest of England, King William I confirmed the earlier agreements made with these ports, which helped him secure the vitally important Strait of Dover. Part of the reason why William's army was able to sail over the Channel from Normandy and land on the Sussex coast relatively unopposed was that the Anglo-Saxon fleet was away off the Yorkshire coast, helping to repel another invasion force from Norway.

The initial importance of the Cinque Ports lay in their situation at the narrowest part of the Channel, which is not only the point of the shortest sea voyage to the Continent but also where the country is most vulnerable to attack and invasion. From 1066 until the early 13th century the Channel was an Anglo-Norman stretch of water with the same king ruling the lands on both sides, and was an important routeway to the 'French' parts of the English monarch's kingdom – Normandy, Aquitaine and Gascony. However, after Normandy was lost to the English Crown in 1204, during the reign of King John (1199-1216), the former allies on either side of the Channel became fierce enemies. Instead of being a waterway between linked kingdoms, the Channel now became a defensive moat between England and the Continent which the Cinque Ports' fleet defended; its waters were frequently a battleground between the Portsmen and unfriendly powers across the sea, and the 13th century became known as 'the violent century in the narrow sea'. The antagonism continued throughout the 14th and 15th centuries with the Hundred Years War between England and France, when many mutual raids involving burning and pillaging took place on both sides of the Channel. The Cinque Ports were repeatedly attacked by the French, and the Portsmen sailed across to France on reprisal raids, or attacked French ships.

In 1205 King John granted the original five Head Ports individual charters in return for their ship service. The earliest known charter granting rights in common to the five ports was that of King Henry II (1154-1189) in 1260, then King Edward I (1272-1307) established the permanent organisational framework of the Confederation of the Cinque Ports with his detailed Great Charter of the Cinque Ports of 1278. Each port in the Confederation had to provide the king with a specified number of vessels for the king's use if requested, each ship to be fully armed and manned with 21 men and a boy, for a period of 15 days each year. The ships might be required to fight on behalf of the Crown as a medieval naval force, but they were also needed to ferry officers of state across the Channel and were frequently called upon by the English kings for the transportation of troops across the sea in times of war.

In return for their ship service the Cinque Ports enjoyed a number of legal and constitutional privileges as well as a considerable degree of self-government. The Ports were not subject to direct taxation, were free of all tolls and customs duties, and were free to trade unhindered by any merchant monopoly – with this long tradition of 'free trading', it is not surprising that many people along the Cinque Ports coast were heavily involved in smuggling in later centuries. Amongst the other special privileges the Cinque Ports enjoyed were the right to seize unclaimed or stolen goods; the 'right of wreck', which meant that any vessel, goods or fish washed ashore must be offered to the Lord Warden of the Cinque Ports; exemption from the jurisdiction of external courts; and the right to hold their own courts and punish offenders in ways that were often specific to the individual ports. Barbaric punishments were common – criminals who had the death penalty imposed in the Cinque Ports were usually executed by drowning, by being tied to a stake and left to the rising tide, but at Sandwich murderers were buried alive, whilst convicted felons at Dover were flung over the cliff overlooking Snargate Street, to the west of the harbour, which was appropriately nicknamed the 'Devil's Drop'.

Also included in the privileges enjoyed by the Portsmen were the rights of 'Den and Strand', which allowed fishermen from the Ports to land their boats at what is now Great Yarmouth on the Norfolk coast in the herring season without paying a fee, to sell their catch without charge, and to dry and mend their nets on the shore. Cinque Ports fishermen had been making an annual visit to the herring fishing grounds off the East Anglian coast for hundreds of years but their problem was to land their catch and get it to market before it went off, so these rights were extremely valuable. The rights of Den and Strand also entitled the Portsmen to run the important annual Herring Fair at Great Yarmouth. The control by Cinque Ports' bailiffs of the lucrative administration and policing of the Fair was bitterly resented in Great Yarmouth, but the privilege continued until it was abolished by King Charles II in the 17th century – a long chapter in the Confederation's history came to an end in 1663 with the last official visit of the Cinque Ports' bailiffs to Great Yarmouth to take charge of the Herring Fair.

The Freemen of the Cinque Ports (the leading citizens of the towns) were always referred to as Barons. The importance of the Cinque Ports to the Crown was recognised by their Barons being granted a special role in the ceremonial of the Coronation, with the duty of holding the canopy over the head of the new monarch during the Coronation procession and the right to attend the Coronation banquet.

The rights and privileges granted to the Portsmen made them very powerful and difficult to control; they became well-nigh ungovernable and were in constant conflict with the Crown. When not busy with ship service duties or fighting invaders, these superb seamen were also prone to piracy, preying on both foreign and English ships in peacetime as well as war. Effective action to reduce their violence and piracy, wrecking and robbery on the high seas proved almost impossible – for example, in the early 14th century Winchelsea was charged with six cases of piracy in the Strait of Dover, despite the town supplying two ships to the Crown to suppress all piracy!

In his Great Charter of 1278 King Edward I formalised the post of Lord Warden of the Cinque Ports, to provide some central authority and control over the unruly Portsmen and act as a link between their interests and the Crown. The Lord Warden became one of the most powerful figures in medieval England, and the holder of the position remained involved with the affairs of the Ports long after the power of the Confederation had declined. For instance, in Dover, when Dover Harbour and the land surrounding it was transferred by Royal Charter to the newly formed Dover Harbour Board in 1606, the then Lord Warden was elected head of the Board. The official residence of the Lord Warden was originally Dover Castle, but in 1708 it was relocated to Walmer Castle, near Deal, one of the defensive artillery forts that King Henry VIII had built along the southern coast of England in the 16th century; Walmer had joined the Confederation in 1353 as a 'limb' of Sandwich, to help that Head Port with its ship service obligations.

The Cinque Ports were of supreme importance to England in the Middle Ages as the main line of defence against foreign invaders, but the Confederation fell into decline from the late 14th century. This was partly due to the growing powers of the Crown in national government, with the monarch becoming increasingly unwilling to brook independent action from any group of towns. Another reason was the silting up of many of the Ports' harbours; the longshore drift of silt, sand and shingle that continues to affect the coastline of south-east England built up bars of shingle and sand that blocked their harbours, or river estuaries silted up, causing the sea to recede and leave once-important ports stranded some distance inland, no longer suitable for any but the smallest vessels, if they were still accessible at all. Of the original five Head Ports of the Confederation, Sandwich is now two miles from the sea, New Romney is high and dry, and the 'old town' of Hythe is a mile inland. Hastings is still sited beside the sea but is now primarily a seaside resort, and only Dover has retained its importance as a port into modern times.

Another reason for the decline of the Confederacy was the creation of a permanent naval fleet in the 16th century, and the subsequent reduction in the ship service required from the Cinque Ports. Action against the Spanish Armada in 1588, during the reign of Queen Elizabeth I, was the last recorded naval engagement in which the Cinque Ports participated – they fitted out and crewed six galleons and supplied five fire ships, which did much damage to the Spanish fleet.

As the need for their ship service diminished, so too did the influence of the Cinque Ports, which eventually lost most of their historic rights and privileges. However, the Confederation still survives today in its modern form. The Cinque Ports Court of Admiralty has jurisdiction over an extensive area of the North Sea and the English Channel, including the busy shipping lanes of the Strait of Dover, and the Lord Warden of the Cinque Ports remains an official post, although it is now purely an honorary and ceremonial position, bestowed by the sovereign in recognition of distinguished service to the State. The Confederation also retains a ceremonial role and the Barons of the Cinque Ports still have a place of honour at the Coronation ceremony, although they no longer carry the canopy over the new monarch during the Coronation procession – that duty was stopped after the Coronation of 1821, when the Barons unfortunately dropped the canopy on King George IV.

This book takes a tour around the 14 towns that make up the present-day Confederation of the Cinque Ports. These are the original five Head Ports of Hastings, New Romney, Hythe, Dover and Sandwich, the Two Ancient Towns of Rye and Winchelsea, and the other seven Corporate Members – Faversham, Folkestone, Margate, Ramsgate, Deal, Tenterden and Lydd.

THE CINQUE PORTS
MISCELLANY

The original five Cinque Ports were selected as being conveniently spaced along the most critical section of the Kent and Sussex coastline. They were equals, though the fact that there is one complete lion on the coat of arms of Hastings against half lions on the coat of arms of the other four Head Ports is said by some to indicate its status as the chief port of the Confederation; however, this is disputed by historians of the other towns, particularly Dover.

Following the Norman Conquest of 1066, King William I had a wooden castle erected at Hastings to protect its harbour, which lay inland on the river estuary. That castle was later replaced by a stone fortress, but much of the structure was destroyed by landslips and coastal erosion in the 13th century, and only a ruined fragment of the castle now crowns West Hill above the town.

Silting began to affect the harbour of Hastings in the 12th century, and the problem was accentuated by the Great Storm of 1287 that damaged much of the south-eastern coast. From the 13th century onwards Hastings declined rapidly as a member of the Confederation of the Cinque Ports; during the reign of King Edward III (1327-77) it was able to send only five ships to assist in the year-long siege of Calais of 1346-47, and to do that had necessitated buying one of the ships from neighbouring Winchelsea. By the 16th century frequent attacks by French raiders and the encroachment of the sea had reduced the once prosperous port of Hastings to poverty. When the wooden pier which gave protection to the harbour was destroyed by a storm, Queen Elizabeth I authorised a collection in 1578 for the building of a replacement; the rebuilding work began in 1595, but such work as was done was swept away by heavy storms in 1597. The new harbour was never built, and Hastings lost its former importance as one of the most powerful of the Cinque Ports.

Following the decline of its harbour, the area of Hastings now called the Old Town developed as a fishing settlement. By 1650, 239 of the 280 heads of households in Hastings were concerned with fishing or services connected with the sea. Modern Hastings is still a fishing town, and Europe's largest beach-launched fishing fleet operates from the eastern end of the beach, where boats are pushed by tractors across the shingle to be launched at high tide, then winched back up the beach on their return.

In the 18th and early 19th centuries many people in Hastings were involved in smuggling, and a number of houses in the Old Town had concealed hiding places where contraband was stored. A contemporary writer described how in one house 'the smuggler's hole is under the floor of the living room, and in several others, many recesses are built in the walls each side of the fireplace, and the opening hidden from view by the cosy seats, and in several others there is an extra double floor, with sufficient space between to take 40-50 tubs; the floor is loosened by a secret spring'. The story of smuggling in the area is now told in The Smuggler's Adventure, a visitor attraction housed in St Clement's Caves deep inside West Hill beneath the ruins of Hastings Castle.

9

Hastings is famous for the unique tall weather-boarded net 'shops', or net drying sheds, clustered beneath East Cliff where local fishermen in the past kept their tackle and dried and stored their nets, as seen in the background of this photograph. There are now 43 net 'shops' but there used to be over 100 of these sheds squeezed onto the narrow strip of land at the edge of the beach. They were built tall and thin so as many fishermen as possible could have a shed on the limited space, and also to save money, since the fishermen had to pay ground rent on the space they occupied. Set amongst the net shops is the town's Fishermen's Museum, housed in the former fishermen's Church of St Nicholas. Inside the museum are many items linked with Hastings' fishing, maritime and boat-building heritage, as well as one of the last of the Hastings Luggers to be built in the town, in 1912; these were clinker-built sailing boats with overlapping planks that could withstand the wear and tear of being hauled over the shingle beach. Several old fishing boats are also on show outside the museum.

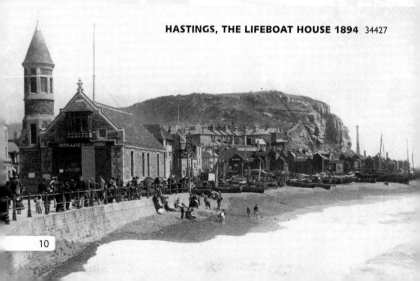

HASTINGS, THE LIFEBOAT HOUSE 1894 34427

**HASTINGS, THE VIEW FROM
THE PIER 1925** 77975

The development of Hastings into a seaside resort began in the
18th century, with people coming there to take the fashionable sea-
water cure for a variety of ailments; this involved drinking copious
amounts of sea-water as well as immersion in the sea. Hotels and
lodging houses were built along the seafront, and by the mid 19th
century Hastings had become a popular resort for everyone, not just
those coming there for the good of their health. Hastings entered the
modern age in 1903 when the town council relaxed its regulations to
allow men and women to bathe from the same beach. However, so
many swimmers now came to Hastings that there were not enough
bathing machines or canvas changing cabins on the beach for them

to change into their bathing costumes, so
the council took the bold step of allowing
'macintosh bathing'. Anyone intending to swim
could arrive at the beach already changed
into a bathing costume, over which he or she
had to wear a macintosh. After the swim, the
swimmer had to put the macintosh back on
and leave the beach. 'Macintosh bathers' were
charged a reduced fee to use the beach from
those using the other beach facilities.

Moving eastwards along the coast and around the headland of Dungeness, we come to New Romney, the second of the five original Head Ports of the Confederation, although it is now an inland settlement over a mile from the sea. New Romney is the 'capital' of the Romney Marsh, a region of flat wetland reclaimed from the sea. The original Anglo-Saxon port and settlement for this region was Old Romney, which was then sited on an island in the estuary of the River Rother. However, Old Romney's harbour silted up and New Romney developed around the mouth of the Rother nearer the sea. New Romney's impressive 12th-century church of St Nicholas in the centre of the town originally stood at the harbourside; ships were moored at the edge of the churchyard, and boat hooks where they used to tie up are still visible on the side walls of the church.

New Romney's decline as a port and the end of its prosperity came in the late 13th century, when a series of severe storms weakened the coastal defences of the area, culminating in the Great Storm of 1287 which flooded the settlement and almost destroyed it, filling the town and its harbour with sand, silt, mud and debris. You can still see evidence of the storm in the tidemark stains on the nave pillars inside St Nicholas's Church. The Great Storm also changed the course of the River Rother to run out into the sea further west, near Rye, which virtually made New Romney an isolated enclave. Its harbour silted up, and ships which had formerly tied up to the walls of the church could no longer sail up the sluggish creek. New Romney had to furnish 5 ships for the king's ship service in the early days of the Confederation, but by the time of the siege of Calais of 1346-77 it could only supply 4 ships. Its importance as a port diminished rapidly during the 14th and 15th centuries after the loss of its harbour, and by the 16th century New Romney was surrounded by choked-up creeks, with the sea over half a mile away. The once-great Cinque Port had become a small inland town.

Traditionally, New Romney is at the centre of the Cinque Ports Confederation – to its west are Hastings, Rye and Winchelsea (the two 'Ancient Towns' that were originally limbs of Hastings, but later became full members of the Confederation), and to its east are Hythe, Dover and Sandwich. Thanks to this central position it became the meeting place of the 'Brotherhood', the Portsmen's own court, where representatives of the Confederation met to regulate its internal affairs and also appoint the Cinque Ports' bailiffs to Great Yarmouth for the annual Herring Fair. The name of the Brotherhood derived from the original meeting place at Brodhull, on the coast near Dymchurch.

New Romney Station is the headquarters of the Romney, Hythe and Dymchurch Railway, a 15-inch-gauge line that opened in 1927 and is the world's smallest public railway service, serving as a commuter train for local schoolchildren as well as a novelty for holidaymakers. The railway runs for 13½ miles along the coastal edge of the Romney Marsh from Dungeness to Hythe, the next Cinque Port in our tour.

DYMCHURCH, THE LIGHT RAILWAY STATION 1927 80405

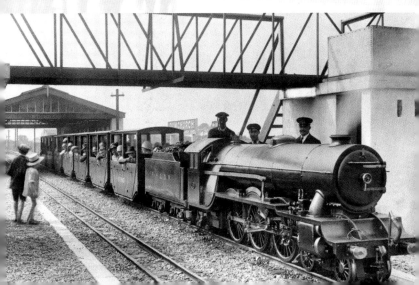

Hythe was the third of the original five Head Ports of the Confederacy, with an obligation to provide 5 ships and 100 men for the King's Ship Service. Hythe means 'haven on the estuary', which was the estuary of a river that used to flow eastwards of the present Romney Marsh, reaching the English Channel near Hythe. By Saxon times the river had turned south to Old Romney, but part of the estuary remained and was used as a harbour for Hythe, where a long-stretched out town developed around it. However, there is no trace left now of Hythe's old harbour.

Hythe's parish church of St Leonard is set on the hillside above the town. Most of the church dates from the 13th century and it is often described as a 'herring church', built when the Cinque Ports enjoyed prosperity from the herring harvest from the sea, linked with the Herring Fair at Great Yarmouth. Hythe's port flourished for some 150 years during the Cinque Ports era, despite many raids by the French in the 14th century – in a particularly devastating attack in 1339, every ship in the harbour was destroyed. Hythe also suffered from the Black Death of the 1340s and storm damage, and then a devastating town fire in 1400. The king actually excused Hythe from ship service for a period, so the town might recover. Then, as in many other places along this coast, Hythe's harbour silted up and the sea receded as shingle was carried eastwards by the process of longshore drift to mass at Hythe and smother the entrance to its haven. By 1450 the old town of Hythe was virtually landlocked, and its harbour facilities were abandoned. By the time of the Spanish Armada in 1588, Hythe could no longer meet its obligations as a Cinque Port.

By Georgian times Hythe had become a market village half a mile inland from the sea. Then in the late 18th century visitors starting coming to a small seaside community that was developing along the coast. By Victorian times a number of hotels had been built facing the beach, and Hythe had become a seaside resort.

On the left of this view is Hythe's Town Hall of 1794, with its ornate clock. Inside the building is a fireplace of 1793 designed by the architect brothers Robert and James Adam, over which is displayed the Banner of the Cinque Ports. Hythe is in the modern local government authority of Shepway District Council, which also includes Folkestone and Romney Marsh. The name comes from the Anglo-Saxon administrative area of the 'lathe of Shepway'. In medieval times the Court of Shepway met a few miles west of Hythe, on Lympe Hill at 'the Shepway crossroads'. This was the principal court of the Cinque Ports Confederation, which met to carry out the official business of the Ports and was the link between the Confederation and central government. On the eastern outskirts of Lympne, at the junction of Aldington Road and the Lympne Hill road to West Hythe, is a monumental cross that was erected in 1923, after the First World War, as a civic war memorial to commemorate the 'DEEDS OF THE MEN OF THE CINQUE PORTS DURING WARTIME'. The memorial was erected at this spot because of its historic link with the Court of Shepway.

HYTHE, HIGH STREET AND THE TOWN HALL 1921 71100

HYTHE, THE PARADE AND MARTELLO TOWERS 1899 44783x

In the early 19th century England was under threat of invasion by the Grande Armée of Napoleon Bonaparte of France, which was massed at Boulogne waiting for favourable weather conditions to cross the Channel. 'All my thoughts are directed towards England', Napoleon had declared in 1803. 'I want only for a favourable wind to plant the Imperial Eagle on the Tower of London.' The Cinque Ports coastline was once again in the forefront of England's defence and a chain of 74 circular forts was built along the coast from Folkestone in Kent to Seaford in East Sussex to prevent an invasion force landing. These squat brick and masonry towers with immensely thick walls and guns on the roof were named Martello Towers after a similar fortification at Cape Mortella in Corsica, which had successfully held off a British attacking force in 1794. None of the Martello Towers ever saw action, as Napoleon eventually turned his attention to campaigns in Egypt and Austria and shelved his plans to invade Britain, but the threat of invasion by his forces remained a continual fear until the defeat of Napoleon at the Battle of Waterloo in 1815. You can see a line of nine Martello Towers along the coast of Hythe Bay in this photograph from 1899. Three of Hythe's towers were demolished in the 19th century to make room for the promenade, but one still stands on Western Parade, converted to a private house, and a handful of derelict towers stand inaccessibly on the MOD firing ranges at Hythe Levels.

Most of the Martello Towers were constructed under the direction of Captain William Ford and General William Twiss of the Royal Engineers. General Twiss also helped with the construction of the Royal Military Canal, another defence against Napoleon's forces, which runs from Seabrook, near Hythe, for 23 miles across the Romney and Walland Marshes to Winchelsea in East Sussex; he is commemorated in Hythe in the names of Twiss Road, Twiss Avenue and Twiss Grove.

The Royal Military Canal was constructed to be an obstacle for invaders and also a means to transport goods, supplies and troops, and was designed so that artillery could be placed to cover every yard of it. The canal was no longer needed for defence purposes following the defeat of Napoleon in 1815, so the government opened it for commercial and public use so they could collect tolls. It was used for the transport of coal and other heavy goods by barge between Hythe and Rye until the coming of the railways killed its trade, and from the 1860s the canal was sold off in sections. Hythe bought its stretch of the canal as an amenity, and it now divides the modern seaside resort of Hythe from the older part of town and remains an ideal place for a punt and a day on the water. Hythe celebrates its canal with the waterborne Venetian Fete every other year, a summer carnival with colourful floating tableaux, illuminated floats and firework displays.

HYTHE, THE CANAL 1918 68153

Dover is the only one of the original five Head Ports of the Confederation to have retained its importance as a port. Its excellent road and rail links to London, large artificial harbour and cross-Channel ferries have given it the name 'Gateway to Britain'.

Dover's position at the narrowest part of the Channel, just 21 miles from France, has always made it strategically important. For centuries it has been defended by the mighty fortress of Dover Castle, 'the lock and key of the kingdom', which was the first concentric castle to be built in Britain. The great keep, inner bailey and much of the curtain wall were built by King Henry II between 1168 and 1186. Additions to the defences were made over succeeding centuries, and the whole stronghold was remodelled during the Napoleonic Wars when great barracks were erected. The chalk cliff below Dover Castle is honeycombed with tunnels and passages. Some were excavated by French troops who unsuccessfully besieged the castle in 1216, and others were created in Napoleonic times to provide cannon ports. The tunnels played a vital part in the Second World War – it was from here in 1940 that the evacuation of Dunkirk was planned, code-named 'Operation Dynamo', and they housed the operations room for Channel Command during the Battle of Britain, the vitally important air campaign fought by the RAF against the German Luftwaffe through the summer and autumn of 1940. The Prime Minister, Winston Churchill, also used rooms in the tunnels as his personal wartime headquarters.

In the 13th century King Edward I decided the post of the Lord Warden of the Cinque Ports should be held by the officer in charge of Dover Castle, the country's strongest land defence, who should also command the Cinque Ports fleet. Hence the office of Lord Warden was conjoined with that of Constable of Dover Castle and Admiral of the Cinque Ports, and Dover Castle became the Lord Warden's official residence. The official residence was relocated to Walmer Castle near Deal in 1708, where it still is today, but the Lord Warden remains the Constable of Dover Castle and Admiral of the Ports, and Dover is where the investiture of a new Lord Warden takes place, a ceremonial event of great pageantry that is now held in the grounds of Dover College.

DOVER, WELLINGTON DOCK AND THE CASTLE c1955 D50011

Dover featured prominently in ship service for the king throughout the Cinque Ports era and its seamen made up an important part of the Confederation fleet in sea battles, starting with the complete defeat of a Danish raiding fleet off Dover and Sandwich in 1069. Dover men played a major role in the crusading fleet that captured Lisbon, on the coast of Portugal, in 1147, and in 1213 they were involved in the great naval victory of the Battle of Damme, fought in the estuary of the River Zwyn in Flanders, when hundreds of French ships were sunk and over 200 were captured, ending a threatened French invasion of England. Dover ships also served in the great naval Battle of Sluys against the French in 1340, one of the opening conflicts of the Hundred Years War, and helped transport the king's armies across the Channel to the Battle of Crecy in 1346 and the Battle of Agincourt in 1415 in the same conflict.

The estuary of the River Dour at Dover was used as a harbour in the Roman period, and the Roman naval fleet operating in Britain, the 'Classis Britannica', was based there for a while. However, the mouth of the Dour had silted up by the Middle Ages, leaving Dover with no natural harbour, and ships had to anchor offshore and unload through small boats. In 1583 the Great Pent was constructed as an enclosed artificial harbour for Dover. The Wellington Dock seen in the photograph on the previous page was the larger successor to that first artificial harbour; it was built in the 1830s and 40s and named after Arthur Wellesley, 1st Duke of Wellington, the victor of the Battle of Waterloo against Napoleon in 1815, who served as Lord Warden of the Cinque Ports from 1829 until 1852. Dover's port grew in importance in the 19th century with the coming of the railways, the development of cross-channel ferries and its designation as a naval base and coaling station. Many enlargements to the harbour and great constructional works were undertaken, and the building of the Admiralty Pier helped free the harbour from blocking by shingle.

DOVER, ADMIRALTY PIER 1901 48058

DOVER, THE CROSS-CHANNEL FERRY TERMINAL 2003 D50703

The Great Admiralty Harbour of 1909 was a vast area of enclosed water designed for both naval and commercial roles. It could provide an anchorage for 13 battleships, 14 cruisers and dozens of naval craft, and a station allowed boat trains carrying ferry passengers to use the pier. Dover expanded its facilities after the Second World War, and its busy harbour is now used for a variety of commercial uses, including the accommodation of large cruise liners as well as the terminals of cross-Channel ferries.

Another way to cross the Channel is to fly across it, and two monuments in Dover commemorate historic flights across the Strait of Dover. One is on the hillside known as Northfall Meadow, immediately behind Dover Castle, where granite paving stones laid out in the shape of a monoplane mark the landing spot of Louis Blériot, the Frenchman who made the very first flight across the Channel from France to England on July 25th 1909. The other is the bronze statue on the Promenade of Charles Rolls, who was a pioneering aviator as well as the founder of the Rolls-Royce car company with Frederick Royce. He made the first non-stop return flight across the Channel from Dover and back in his Wright Flyer biplane on 2nd June 1910, but unfortunately he was killed a few weeks later when his plane crashed during a flying display near Bournemouth, which also made him the first Briton to die in an aviation accident. The statue was unveiled in 1912 and was the work of Kathleen Scott, the sculptress wife of the Antarctic explorer Captain Robert Falcon Scott.

Sandwich was once a thriving port on the River Stour, and the most easterly of the original five Head Ports of the Confederation. The Anglo-Saxon King Edward the Confessor (1042-1066) made its harbour a base for his fleet. Following the Norman Conquest, the Domesday survey of 1086 showed that Sandwich was the second largest town in Kent after Canterbury. During its medieval peak Sandwich was considered second only to London as an entry port to England, able to handle up to 600 ships at any one time, and was also the country's chief naval and military port of the period.

In 1217 a Cinque Ports fleet sailed out of Sandwich and engaged a large number of French ships in battle off the nearby coast; the French vessels were bringing reinforcements to the invasion force of Louis Capet, son of the French king, that had come to England the previous year in alliance with a group of English barons in rebellion against King John. The Portsmen catapulted pots of finely powdered quicklime at their opponents, blinding them in the resultant clouds of fine dust and allowing easy boarding of the French ships by the English. The Battle of Sandwich was a decisive victory that removed the threat of a French invasion for several years. Some of the booty from the captured French ships was used to finance the building of St Bartholomew's Hospital in Sandwich, a chapel and almshouse accommodation for 16 elderly people that still stands in Dover Road – the battle had been fought on St Bartholomew's Day, 24th August, and it was believed that the saint had given victory to the English.

By the 14th century, most Cinque Ports were protected by walls or ramparts as a defence against the constant threat of French raids from the sea. Much of Sandwich's town wall has now disappeared, but you can still walk around some of the remaining earthworks of the medieval defences. The Fishergate is the only fortified gateway into the medieval walled town that has survived; built of flint near the quayside in 1384, it was one of the main entrances to Sandwich from the riverside wharves through the narrow and cobbled Quay Lane, which led to the Custom House.

SANDWICH, THE FISHERGATE
1894 34209

SANDWICH, THE BARBICAN AND THE BRIDGE 1894 34211

An additional defence for Sandwich was the Barbican, which King Henry VIII had built in 1539. It later became the residence of the keepers of the toll bridge over the River Stour in front of the building, where tolls were charged until 1977.

The port of Sandwich prospered until the 15th century when its harbour began to silt up. Although King Henry VII (1485-1509) was able to call on 95 ships with 1,500 sailors from Sandwich for the king's service, by the 16th century Sandwich Haven had silted up so badly that the commercial future of the town was in jeopardy. Help was sought from King Henry VIII who visited Sandwich in 1532 and 1539, staying at the fine timber-framed house now called The King's Lodging (or Old King's House) in Strand Street, but nothing was done. Fresh hopes were raised when Queen Elizabeth I visited in 1573 and was sumptuously wined and dined with a banquet of 160 courses before being petitioned to take some action concerning the silting up of Sandwich Haven. Despite the queen being 'very merry', no help was forthcoming, and the port continued to slide into decline.

Following the decline of its port, Sandwich reinvented itself as a cloth-weaving town when Flemish Huguenot (Protestant) refugees settled there in the 16th century after fleeing religious persecution following Spanish conquests in the Low Countries. They brought their skills in weaving cloth to Sandwich, and developed a thriving business in the town with English wool. They also affected its architectural style, as a number of properties in Sandwich exhibit Flemish features: good examples are the Dutch House in King Street, White Friars in New Street and the tower of St Peter's Church, which was rebuilt by the Huguenot community after it collapsed in 1661 and was topped with the Flemish-style cupola seen in the background of the photograph on the opposite page.

Sandwich now lies well inland from the coast, and although the distance from the sea is only two miles, the meanders of the Stour mean a vessel must make a trip of nearly eight miles upriver to tie up at Sandwich Quay. Despite the silting up of its harbour, some commercial shipping still visited Sandwich until the early 20th century, although the increasing size of mercantile ships eventually killed off its seaborne trade. The Thames sailing barges seen in this view of 1924 may have been carrying coal, timber, salt and other commodities between here and London, or other east coast ports. The merchant shipping of the past has now given way to small pleasure boats that ply the Stour.

SANDWICH, THE RIVER 1924 76227

By the late 12th century Hastings had become the first of the Head Ports to suffer from the problem that has subsequently faced all the Cinque Port towns – the process of longshore drift, in which local wave and wind currents gradually drive shingle and sand eastwards along the Channel coast. The harbour at Hastings was blocking up, and the town had to recruit two neighbouring ports to help it meet its ship service obligations and preserve its privileges. These were Rye and Winchelsea, which in the Middle Ages were coastal ports although they are both some distance inland now, and they were attached to the Cinque Port of Hastings as 'limbs'. By the mid 14th century both Rye and Winchelsea had become such busy and prosperous ports that they were admitted into the Confederation as full members in their own right, with the title of 'Ancient Towns', having complete equality in all respects with the original five Head Ports. With the addition of Rye and Winchelsea, the Confederation took the new title of 'The Cinque Ports and the Two Ancient Towns', the name by which it is still known today.

RYE, THE RIVER ROTHER 1901 47445

In the Middle Ages Rye was a thriving port sited on a hill above the estuary of the River Rother, with a fishing fleet and a wharf where the king's galleys were docked and repaired. In 1289 Rye contributed five ships to the Cinque Port fleet, as many as Hythe, Sandwich and New Romney were providing. However, from the 14th century onwards the sea retreated as the estuary silted up, and Rye is now an inland town with the Rother joining the open sea nearly three miles away.

Rye suffered frequent attacks by the French and in 1249 a castle was built as part of its defences. In the 15th century the castle became the home of the d'Ypres family, thus its present name of Ypres Tower; it is now one of the sites of the Rye Castle Museum. Further defences were added to Rye in the 14th century, including the Landgate, the only survivor of four medieval gates into the walled town. Built in the north-east of the town to provide defence on the landward side, it originally had a drawbridge and a portcullis, and gates which were closed at dusk each day.

The worst attack by the French on Rye was in 1377, when all but the stone buildings of the town were burnt down, and a number of people were killed. Rye's parish church of St Mary at the southern end of Lion Street had to be rebuilt after its roof caught fire and collapsed during the attack, which allowed the raiders to pounce on the church bells and carry them off to France. In true Portsmen fashion, men from Rye and Winchelsea sailed over to France on a daring reprisal raid the following year and retrieved the bells, along with much other loot that had been taken. One of the recovered bells was then hung in Watchbell Street, where it was rung in times of danger and to warn inhabitants of approaching French raids; the bell was not returned to the church until the 16th century.

The decline of Rye's port over the centuries, as the river estuary silted up and the sea retreated, left the town with very limited harbour facilities. The local people had to look for another sort of living and the answer was smuggling, which took over Rye's economy to such an extent that by the 18th century the town was called the smuggling capital of England. Big cargo ships could no longer reach Rye, but smaller smugglers' vessels could sail up the Rother and unload their contraband. Smuggling was a very profitable trade due to the swingeing taxes imposed on imported goods such as wine, brandy, tobacco. spices, silks and lace, and many townspeople were involved with it. Contraband goods were often hidden in the attics of houses, which at that time were not divided between individual dwellings so could also be used by people trying to evade the Revenue men – they could go up to an attic in one part of the town and come down in a completely different area. The smugglers also stored their goods in the cavernous old cellars that lie beneath some of the town's houses and other buildings.

One of the most famous smugglers' haunts in Rye was the 15th-century Mermaid Inn in Mermaid Street, which in medieval times led down to the harbour. Its cellars were used as a store for contraband, and the inn was a regular meeting place of the Hawkhurst Gang, the most notorious and ruthless smugglers in Kent and Sussex, who caroused with their cocked and loaded pistols close to hand on the tables. Smuggling has been much romanticised in recent times, but smugglers treated informers against them with brutality and the Hawkhurst Gang were no exception. In an incident in 1747, gang members murdered a customs officer and a man who had identified one of their number to him in horrific ways – the officer was beaten until he was near to death and then buried alive in a fox earth, and the informer was suspended down a dry well, stoned and left to starve to death. Seven members of the gang were convicted of the murders and six were hanged, one having died in gaol.

Smuggling continued to flourish in Rye up to the first half of the 19th century. Then, along with the policy of Free Trade, came the abolition of most customs duties. This, together with the reform of the customs service in 1853 to provide a more efficient force, caused the smuggling trade to wither. Rye again had to find a new way to make a living, and it was tourism that provided the town with continued prosperity. Rye has kept its medieval plan almost intact, and its streets (some still cobbled) are lined with beautiful old buildings, many timber-framed and dating from the 15th to the 17th centuries; an example is Hartshorne House, the handsome three-gabled house on the right of this view, which is also known as the Old Hospital because sick soldiers were housed there during the Napoleonic Wars. Rye became a magnet for Victorian excursionists in search of the picturesque, and it still attracts thousands of tourists each year. Present-day Rye is a charming and attractive town, but if you want to see how it looked in Victorian times, there is a wonderful scale model of Rye in the 19th century in the town's Heritage Centre.

RYE, MERMAID STREET 1888 21161

Winchelsea was once the major port of medieval Sussex, but its harbour silted up and the coastline receded, and it is now an inland settlement. The original Winchelsea was on a shingle spit running north-east from the Fairlight Cliffs that was broken up by a series of storms in the 13th century. The town was gradually being washed away, and in 1281 King Edward I ordered a new settlement to be built on higher ground, on land that he personally provided. 'New' Winchelsea was laid out as a planned 'new town' on a sandstone outcrop which projected into the estuary of the River Brede. Old Winchelsea was finally engulfed by the sea in the Great Storm of 1287. The resettled migrants from the flooded town moved into their new town in 1288 and were offered their rectangular house plots rent free for the first seven years. New Winchelsea was surrounded by a town wall and four fortified gateways, three of which are still standing. The Strand Gate protected the entrance from the harbour on the River Brede at the bottom of Strand Hill. It was the main entrance into the town in medieval times, and still is today.

WINCHELSEA, STRAND GATE
c1960 WI06005

WINCHELSEA, THE COURT HALL 1894 34452

New Winchelsea retained Old Winchelsea's affiliation to the Cinque Ports as a limb of Hastings. It became a full member of the Confederation in the mid 14th century, as one of the two Ancient Towns, by which time it was sending a quota of 21 ships manned by 596 men to the Cinque Ports fleet, eclipsing even Dover's quota of 16 ships and 336 men.

One of the oldest houses in Winchelsea is the 14th-century building now called the Court Hall. This was originally the home of Gervase Alard, who in 1295 became the first recorded mayor of the new town and in 1300 was appointed Captain and Admiral of the Western Fleet. The Court Hall is now the headquarters of the Corporation of Winchelsea, which is the smallest town in the country to have its own corporation and mayor. The corporation lost its civil and judicial powers under the Municipal Corporations Act of 1883, but was uniquely allowed to remain in existence as an 'exempt charity' outside the modern structure of local government, to maintain Winchelsea's membership of the Confederation of the Cinque Ports.

Winchelsea began to decline in the mid 14th century, triggered by the disruption to its trade caused by the Hundred Years War with France, the depredations of the Black Death and damage inflicted by several devastating French raids on the town. However, the most serious problem was the blocking up of its harbour, partly through the eastward drift of silt and shingle and subsequent receding of the sea, and partly because the infilling of the upper reaches of the River Brede to create new farm land had reduced the flow of the river and its scouring effect on the harbour. By the 16th century there was no access by ship to Winchelsea, and it had ceased to be a port.

King Edward I's new town of the 1280s had been laid out on a grid-iron pattern of four streets by four streets at right angles with 39 blocks, but over the years the inhabitants of the medieval town moved out as its trade declined, and the buildings were left to crumble and decay. Present-day Winchelsea now covers only 12 of the original 39 blocks and is a mere shadow of what once stood there. Outcrops of old stonework occur around the town, and crop marks in the fields west of the church are evidence that foundations of further buildings lie hidden beneath the turf.

Winchelsea today is an attractive small town with houses that are architecturally mostly 17th-, 18th and 19th-century, but beneath many of these houses are the stone-vaulted cellars of earlier dwellings that stood on these sites in medieval times. These medieval cellars, or undercrofts, were used for storing the wine imported from Gascony that formed the basis of the medieval town's trade – Winchelsea was one of the ten major wine-importing ports of England in the Middle Ages. Around 30 of these medieval cellars are currently accessible, but the existence of many more is known. It has been estimated from records showing the amount of wine coming into Winchelsea in 1300/01 that there could have been as many as 70 cellars around the town in its Cinque Port heyday, with the average cellar holding over 120 hogsheads (6,300 gallons) of wine.

Ship service was an onerous duty, and the increased demands on the Cinque Ports fleet following the loss of Normandy to the English Crown in the early 13th century, together with the problems caused by the silting up of some of their harbours, imposed a severe strain on the resources of the original five Head Ports; consequently they enlisted the help of neighbouring settlements to help them fulfil their ship service obligations. These places were known as 'members', or 'limbs'. Hastings had already enlisted the help of Rye and Winchelsea as 'limbs' in 1191 (both places were later admitted to the Confederation as full members, as the 'Two Ancient Towns'), but between the 12th and 15th centuries many more limbs were recruited to assist the Cinque Ports and the Two Ancient Towns with their obligations, which were administered as outlying parts of their Head Port. Due to the vagaries of the historical records the full number of limbs is not clear, but there may have been as many as 42 places involved in the Confederation.

The limbs were drawn from an extensive area, from Seaford in Sussex to Brightlingsea on the Essex coast, which was a limb of Sandwich and the only town associated with the Confederation that is not in Kent or Sussex. Some limbs were small villages which as 'non-corporate' members negotiated directly with their Head Port to provide ships and men in return for the right to share in its privileges. Others were more substantial communities and were granted their own charters by the Crown as 'corporate members'. Over the centuries some limbs became larger and more important than their Head Port, but none were ever permitted to become Head Ports in the Confederation.

A full account of all the towns and villages involved in the Confederation as corporate and non-corporate limbs in its history is beyond the scope of this small book, so we will now briefly tour the seven places that are the corporate members of the Confederation of the Cinque Ports in its modern form. In company with the original five Head Ports and Two Ancient Towns of Hastings, New Romney, Hythe, Dover, Sandwich, Rye and Winchelsea, the present-day Confederation includes the seven corporate members of Faversham, Folkestone, Margate, Tenterden, Ramsgate, Deal and Lydd.

FAVERSHAM, WEST STREET c1960 F13038

Faversham is sited at the head of a tidal creek in the Swale borough of north Kent and had a busy port and shipbuilding industry in the Middle Ages, when it was known as 'the King's Port'. In later centuries its quay was bustling with Thames barges exporting locally grown produce to London, but it now mainly harbours pleasure craft. Faversham joined the Confederation in 1252 as a limb of Dover, which often supported the town in its disputes with successive abbots of Faversham Abbey. The abbey stood to the north-east of the town but was dissolved in 1538 and its buildings were demolished. The abbey site was given to Sir Thomas Cheney, Lord Warden of the Cinque Ports from 1536 to 1558, who set up a venture with Faversham's mayor, Thomas Arden, to sell the stone from the demolished abbey and ship it out from the town's quay; much of it was taken to France and used to strengthen the fortifications of the Pale of Calais, the last remaining English territory in France and England's Continental bridgehead until it was lost during the reign of Queen Mary I (1553-58). This photograph shows West Street, lined with historic houses, which connects the town with Faversham Creek.

Folkestone also became a limb of Dover in the 13th century, with the obligation to supply seven boats to help Dover meet its ship service requirements. The original settlement of Folkestone was the part now called the Old Town, which developed through fishing and its closeness to the Continent as a landing place and trading port. However, there was no natural harbour, and boats were drawn up and loaded and unloaded on the beach. Over the centuries there were several attempts to build a harbour at Folkestone, but problems of silting up and the destruction wrought by storms meant that constant repair, maintenance and rebuilding were required. In 1635 it was announced by the local corporation that at the beat of a drum or 'sufficient warning', every householder within the town, or some other fit person in their stead, 'should repair the said harbour, each of them provided with shovelled or other fitting and meete tooles or instruments for the clearinge, scouringe, and expulsinge of the beach out of the said haven or harbour'. Unfortunately, despite this and other 'calls to arms', the battle was a losing one. Erosion by the sea continually put paid to attempts at harbour building and maintenance, and Folkestone fell into a long period of decline until it eventually got a proper harbour in the 19th century.

In the late 18th and early 19th centuries Folkestone was a particular hotbed of the smuggling that was rife all along the south-eastern coast, and had a reputation for lawlessness, wild behaviour and general disrespect for law and authority. An example of why this reputation was well deserved occurred in 1820, after eleven smugglers from Folkestone were caught bringing contraband across the Channel and taken to Dover Gaol. Folkestone fishermen, their wives and supporters marched to Dover and stormed the gaol. Soldiers despatched from Dover Castle stood helplessly by as the mob tore down the gaol brick by brick and released all the men, who disappeared into the countryside and made their way back to Folkestone. No attempt at recapturing them was made.

FOLKESTONE, PADDLE STEAMERS IN THE HARBOUR 1906 53473

Folkestone finally got a properly constructed harbour in the 19th century. The subsequent development of cross-Channel paddle steamer ferry services and the coming of the South Eastern Railway propelled Folkestone into its Victorian and Edwardian heyday by bringing ferry passengers to the town as well as stimulating its growth into 'Fashionable Folkestone', a stylish and rather exclusive seaside resort. Large hotels were built around the harbour and along the cliff top, as well as amenities to cater for the holiday-making public, such as a pleasure pier (demolished in 1954), a bathing establishment and theatres. In 1885 the water-powered Cliff Lift made its debut, allowing visitors to travel with ease between The Leas, the mile-long promenade at the top of the West Cliff, and Lower Sandgate Road and the seafront. Seen on the right of the photograph on the opposite page in 1901, the Cliff Lift still operates today, working by the simple 'water balance' system – as a chamber at the base of one lift fills with water it descends, sending the other up the cliff top, like a see-saw.

The Leas was the fashionable place to see and be seen in Victorian and Edwardian Folkestone. Only respectable appearance and behaviour were tolerated on the elegant promenade, which was patrolled by 'beadles', the local landowner Lord Radnor's own policemen – a man could be turned off The Leas for not wearing a tie, and swearing was an arrestable offence that could result in a fine, or even a night in gaol.

The Cinque Ports were used as embarkation ports for transporting armies across the Channel throughout the medieval and Tudor periods, and that tradition continued in Folkestone during the First World War of the early 20th century, when it became the main port of embarkation for troops going off to fight in France and Flanders. Around 7 million men marched down the road to the harbour on their way to war and the horrors of the trenches, many never to return. After the war a striking memorial was erected at the eastern end of The Leas and the road down which the troops marched was renamed the Road of Remembrance, in commemoration of the men who never came home.

FOLKESTONE, THE LEAS FROM THE PIER 1901 48054

Margate became a limb of Dover in 1229, and played a full part in the Confederation's ship service requirements – for instance, records show the town supplied 15 ships and 160 men to King Edward III to assist in the year-long siege of Calais of 1346-47.

Margate remained a small fishing port until the early 18th century, when it developed into the country's first commercial sea-bathing resort. Visitors came there to take the newly-popular 'sea-water cure' which doctors were advocating as the panacea for many illnesses and diseases. Margate became very popular with the rich and fashionable set through its easy access by boat from London, and many visitors travelled there on 'hoys' – these were flat-bottomed boats that carried both passengers and cargo along the coast and on the Thames, and it is from these boats that the nautical cry of 'Ahoy' originated, which was used to hail a hoy to stop and take on a passenger. Margate's exclusiveness ended in the 19th century when cheap rail and paddle steamer fares allowed Londoners to flock there and enjoy its entertainments in such numbers that it was called 'London by the Sea'. With its nine miles of glorious sandy beaches, Margate remains a popular seaside resort.

MARGATE, THE HARBOUR 1906 54762

MARGATE, DONKEYS ON THE SANDS
1906 54759

Bathing machines are lined up on Margate's beach in the background of this view, which were used for people to change into their bathing apparel and conserve their modesty whilst they took a dip in the sea. These small huts on wheels were backed into the sea by horses, and the people wishing to bathe then disembarked down steps at the rear of the vehicles. Bathing machines were a feature of seaside resorts all round Britain in the 19th century but they were invented in Margate by a local man, Benjamin Beale, in the 1750s. Most people bathed naked in those early days, and Mr Beale's original design had a canvas hood over the steps that shielded the bather from prying eyes; the hood was dispensed with in later years, with the increasing use of bathing costumes.

Margate also lays claim to have been the first resort to offer donkey rides as a seaside amusement – from about 1800 a Mr Bennett in the High Street kept donkeys for hire at a shilling an hour. In the early days of the resort Margate's donkeys were described as 'carrying angels by day and spirits by night' – a reference to their secondary night-time use by local smugglers to carry contraband away from the beach.

RAMSGATE, HARBOUR PARADE AND NEW ROAD c1920 68467

Ramsgate became a limb of Sandwich in 1483, but in less than
200 years it had eclipsed its Head Port in importance as a sea port,
particularly fostering trade with Russia and the Baltic countries.
Work on building Ramsgate's present harbour began in 1749 and
it was completed around 1850. The outer harbour was constructed
as a 'harbour of refuge' to provide a safe haven for shipping in bad
weather; the West Pier lighthouse has the Latin words 'perfugium
miseris' cut into the stonework below its lantern, meaning 'shelter
for the distressed'. The tidal ball on its mast is seen on the skyline in
the centre of this photograph, which was raised and lowered by the
duty Dockmaster according to the tides. When the ball was at the
top of the mast it denoted that there was more than 10 feet of water
between the pier heads of the outer harbour, indicating to shipping
that there was enough water to safely enter the harbour.

In 1821 King George IV used Ramsgate as his point of embarkation and return for a journey to Hanover; the warm send off and reception home that he was given by the local people so delighted him that he ordered Ramsgate to be termed a 'Royal Harbour', the only one in mainland Britain. In 1823 a tall, pointed obelisk was erected near the harbour to commemorate this – it is known locally as the Royal Toothpick.

Ramsgate's Clock House is seen in the background on the right of this photograph, which now houses the Maritime Museum. The Clock House is where the Ramsgate Meridian Line is situated, from which the town's own particular Mean Time was calculated in the past and used by mariners to set their chronometers before setting sail. Ramsgate Mean Time is 5 minutes and 41 seconds ahead of the world standard Greenwich Mean Time. Although Ramsgate adopted Greenwich Mean Time in 1848 to be in line with the rest of the country, Ramsgate Mean Time is still officially recognised by Greenwich, a unique distinction that makes Ramsgate the only town in Britain to have its own Mean Time.

RAMSGATE, THE HARBOUR CROSSWALL 1907 58287

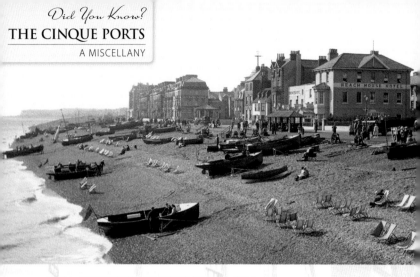

DEAL, THE BEACH, LOOKING SOUTH 1924 76046x

Deal became a limb of Sandwich in the 13th century. The stretch of water between the coastline near Deal and the treacherous Goodwin Sands provides a naturally sheltered anchorage where sailing ships used to anchor up in bad weather, often re-supplying whilst they were there. This sheltered position allowed Deal to become an important shipping and military port even though it had no harbour or berthing facilities – goods and passengers were transferred from ship to shore using smaller tender craft. As steam gradually replaced sail from the mid 19th century, fewer ships needed to anchor off Deal; the town developed a tourism industry as its maritime trade declined, and Deal became the popular and elegant seaside resort that it remains today.

The building in the centre of this view, surmounted with what looks like a cross with a large ball at its base, is the Timeball Tower. From 1855 until 1927 the timeball dropped down the shaft above the tower at exactly 1pm GMT every day to help mariners on passing ships keep accurate time. The Timeball Tower is now a museum that tells the story of the role of the building in Deal's history, and explains why timekeeping was so important for shipping in the past.

St Leonard's Church in Upper Deal, at the junction of Rectory Road and Manor Road, is the parish church of Deal and the oldest church in the town, although much altered and extended over the years. Its tower was rebuilt in the 17th century and topped with a distinctive cupola to act as a navigational aid for shipping approaching the Goodwin Sands. One of several galleries added to the church to create more space is known as the Pilots' Gallery, partly because the pilots who worked in Deal used to sit there during services, and partly because the gallery as seen today was rebuilt by the pilots themselves in the early 18th century, after a battle with the church authorities to retain the right to use it as a place reserved for their worship. There was always a possibility that the pilots might be called out to attend shipping during services, and this private gallery allowed them discreet exit from the church without disturbing the rest of the congregation. The gallery is decorated with paintings of pilots in the traditional uniform of the period, wearing tricorn hats and holding spyglasses.

DEAL, ST LEONARD'S CHURCH
1906 56922

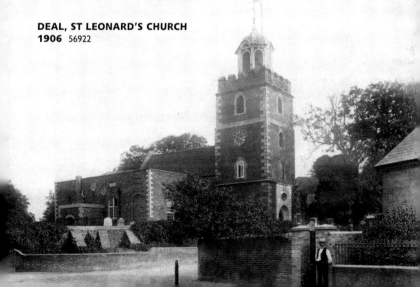

Tenterden became a limb of Rye in 1449, supplying one ship and crew each year to assist its Head Port with its ship service requirements. In the Middle Ages the River Rother linked Tenterden to the sea, and there was a harbour as well as an important shipbuilding industry at Small Hythe, within the Hundred of Tenterden a short distance south of the town. However, as in so many other places, the silting up of the Rother and coastal changes over the centuries caused Tenterden to lose access to the sea, and it is now some ten miles from the coast. Under the terms of the charter granting Tenterden membership of the Confederation, the local government of the town from then on was to be by Jurats and an elected Bailiff. The first Bailiff elected in 1449 was Thomas Pittlesden, whose personal coat of arms is shown on the mizzen mast of the ship on Tenterden's coat of arms that appears on the town sign, shown in the illustration on page 2 of this book; the coat of arms on the main sail of the ship is that of the Cinque Ports Confederation itself.

TENTERDEN, HIGH STREET 1900 44994

Lydd is located on the Denge Marsh that adjoins the Romney Marsh on the western side of Kent, and joined the Confederation as a limb of New Romney. In the Middle Ages Lydd was on an island in Rye Bay, but longshore drift eventually connected the island to the mainland and Lydd is now an inland settlement. Lydd's position on the Romney Marsh made it a base for smuggling in the past and there are several smugglers' graves in the churchyard of its fine medieval All Saints' Church, as well as graves of sailors who were shipwrecked off the Dungeness headland. The churchyard is also the resting place of Lt Thomas Edgar RN, who served as master on the 'Discovery' that accompanied Captain James Cook on the 'Resolution' on his third voyage of exploration to the Pacific; it was on this voyage that Captain Cook was killed by natives in Hawaii in 1779. When Lt Edgar ended his seagoing days he came to Dungeness where he became keeper of the Dungeness Signal Tower, and remained in that post until his death in 1801. His grave in Lydd's churchyard is now marked with a stone plaque in the ground, and his original tombstone is preserved in the North Chapel inside the church for safekeeping. The inscription on the tombstone is badly weathered and hard to read, but records that Lt Edgar came into the Navy at 10 years of age and 'sailed round the world with the unfortunate Captain Cook'. There was also a poem inscribed on the lower part of the tombstone which is now so weathered it is impossible to decipher, but a transcription from an archive source has been posted on the website of the Captain Cook Society (www.captaincooksociety.com); its words could be true of any Cinque Port sailor:

> *Tom Edgar at last has sailed out of this world,*
> *His shroud is put on and his topsails are furl'd*
> *He lies in death's boat without any concern,*
> *And is moor'd for a full due ahead and astern,*
> *Ov'r the compass of life he has merrily run,*
> *His voyage is completed, his reckoning is done.*

SPORTING CINQUE PORTS

Sandwich is famous for its trio of golf courses around Sandwich Bay, most notably the Royal St George. Founded in 1887, this course is widely regarded as one of the finest in the world, and regularly hosts the British Open Golf Championships. The famous writer Ian Fleming often frequented the Royal St George, which he wrote about under the name of Royal St Mark's as the setting for the memorable game of golf between James Bond, 007 and Auric Goldfinger in his book 'Goldfinger'.

People come to Dover from all over the world to swim across the Channel to France, the 'Everest' of long-distance open-water swimming. The first person to successfully accomplish the feat of swimming across the Strait of Dover was Captain Matthew Webb in 1875, whose achievement made him a national celebrity; he dived into the Channel off the Admiralty Pier at Dover, and he finally arrived on the French coast, at Calais, 21 hours and 45 minutes later. A memorial to Captain Webb in the form of a bronze bust on a stone plinth stands on Dover's seafront near the harbour.

DOVER 1906 56938

HAUNTED CINQUE PORTS

The Theatre Royal in Addington Street in Margate is said to be one of the most haunted theatres in southern England. Many strange phenomena have been reported there, including the sounds of whispering when no one else is there, disembodied footsteps and mysterious balls of light that move across the stage. The building is also said to be haunted by the ghost of Sarah Thorne, who famously managed the Theatre Royal in the 19th century and made it celebrated throughout the south of England. She died in 1899 but her shade is said to have roamed the building since 1918, possibly in protest at it being used for various non-theatrical purposes at various times over the 20th century, which included a role as a bingo hall.

Offshore from Deal is the treacherous sandbank of the Goodwin Sands which has caused more than 2,000 shipwrecks, including that of the 'Lady Lovibond' in February 1748; according to legend, the first mate deliberately steered the ship onto the sandbank in a fit of jealous rage because the captain had brought his new bride on board, with whom he was also in love. The 'Lady Lovibond' is said to reappear near Goodwin Sands every 50 years from the date it was wrecked, as a ghost ship. The first sighting of the phantom ship, in 1798, was reported by two separate vessels; a sighting in 1848 appeared so real that a lifeboat was sent out to look for survivors; she was seen again in 1898, and then in 1948, when a ship's captain described the vessel as having an eerie green glow; however, there was no reported sighting when it was next due, in 1998.

Dover Castle is said to be haunted by the rather gruesome spectre of Sean Flynn, a 15-year-old army drummer boy who was stationed at the castle during the Napoleonic Wars. One night he was sent into the town on an errand; knowing that he was carrying a large amount of money, two soldiers ambushed him outside the castle, robbed him of the money and murdered him by cutting off his head. His headless ghost is said to walk around the battlements of the castle at dead of night, beating his drum – the sound of his ghostly drumming has been heard by those with ears to listen...

QUIZ QUESTIONS

Answers on page 52.

1. Standing within the walls of Dover Castle next to the ancient church of St Mary in Castro is the strange structure seen in the photograph below. What is it?

2. Why does the Mayor of Sandwich wear black robes on all ceremonial occasions?

3. Buried in the churchyard of St Leonard's Church at Hythe is Lionel Lukin (1742-1834). The inscription on his tombstone proudly claims that he was the inventor of – what?

4. What and where in Rye is the Enchantress Tower?

5. Only one woman has ever held the position of Lord Warden of the Cinque Ports – who was she?

DOVER, ST MARY IN CASTRO CHURCH c1874 7081

HASTINGS, ST CLEMENT'S CHURCH c1955 H36041

6. Which member of the Cinque Ports Confederation has an explosive past?

7. A plaque in Augusta Gardens in Folkestone marks where Samuel Plimsoll lived from 1895 until his death in 1898; he is buried in the graveyard of St Martin's Church at Cheriton. The plaque was presented by the National Union of Seamen and erected by the New Folkestone Society. Samuel Plimsoll is remembered as 'The Sailor's Friend' – why?

8. Many people in the Romney Marsh region were involved in an activity known as 'owling' in the past – what was this?

9. Where and what along the Cinque Ports coastline is Samphire Hoe?

10. St Clement's Church in the Old Town of Hastings has two strange round objects set into the stonework of its tower on the wall facing the sea, on either side of the belfry louvre, as seen in the photograph above. What are they?

RECIPE

DOVER SOLE WITH FRESH HERBS

Today's fishermen of the Cinque Ports coast mainly operate from small day boats fishing the English Channel. Their most valuable catches are sea bass, cod, lobster, and various varieties of sole, including the delicious Dover sole – this fish is not exclusively found at Dover, but probably got its name because that was the port where it was landed in quantity and from where it was transported to the London markets. Dover sole is best cooked very simply so that its fine, delicate flavour can be enjoyed. Serves 4.

> 4 Dover sole, with the fins and dark skin removed
>   (the white skin should be left on, and can be eaten)
> 2-3 tablespoonfuls of seasoned plain flour
> 3 tablespoonfuls of olive oil
> 25g/1oz unsalted butter
> Juice of 1 lemon
> 1 tablespoonful finely chopped fresh herbs,
>   such as tarragon, dill, parsley

Coat both sides of the fish in the seasoned flour. Heat the oil in a large, wide, non-stick frying pan. Cook the fish one or two at a time over a medium heat for a few minutes on each side, until they are golden brown and cooked through, then keep them warm whilst the others are cooking. Add the butter to the remaining oil in the pan and heat until it has melted. Stir in the lemon juice and the chopped fresh herbs and mix it all together. Pour the buttery sauce over the fish and serve immediately.

RECIPE

SUSSEX HEAVIES

This is an old traditional recipe from Sussex for small, fruity cakes that are best eaten on the same day as baking, and are especially nice eaten hot, straight from the oven. This should make about 12 Heavies.

> 225g/8oz self-raising flour
> A pinch of salt
> 25g/1oz caster sugar
> 50g/2oz butter or margarine
> 50g/2oz currants or raisins, or a mixture of both
> 175ml/6fl oz sour milk, or fresh milk 'soured' with
>   the juice of half a lemon
> A little extra caster sugar to finish

Pre-heat the oven to 220°C/425°F/Gas Mark 7 and grease a baking sheet.

Mix the flour, salt and sugar in a bowl. Rub in the butter or margarine until the mixture resembles fine breadcrumbs, then mix in the dried fruit. Mix to a soft dough with as much of the liquid as is necessary (reserve the rest).

Roll out the dough gently on a floured surface to about 2.5cms (1 inch) thick, and cut it into rounds about 5cms (2 inches) in diameter. Place the rounds on greased baking sheets, brush with the remaining sour milk and sprinkle with a little extra caster sugar. Bake near the top of the pre-heated oven for about 10 minutes, until golden brown.

QUIZ ANSWERS

1. The octagonal structure next to the church is the weatherworn shell of the 'pharos', or lighthouse, one of two lighthouses that the Romans erected in Dover in the 2nd century AD as beacons for their galleys coming into the harbour. (The other pharos on the Western Heights survives only at the level of its foundations.) It is the tallest surviving Roman building in Britain, although the top storey was rebuilt in the 15th century.

2. In 1457, some 4,000 Frenchmen from Honfleur landed at Sandwich and laid waste to the town. Many citizens were killed, including the mayor, John Drury. Since then, successive mayors of Sandwich have always worn black ceremonial robes in memory of the event, a tradition that continues to this day despite attempts by Honfleur (now twinned with Sandwich) to persuade the town to drop the custom.

3. Lionel Lukin was a Hythe coach-builder who is credited as the inventor of the first self-righting lifeboat. He began to experiment with designs for an 'unimmergible' lifeboat in 1784, and took out a patent in 1785. In 1786 he was asked by Dr John Sharpe, Archdeacon of Northumberland, to convert a coble which included the principles of his patent, and that boat served for a number of years at Bamburgh as the first purpose-built lifeboat. Lukin's tombstone in St Leonard's churchyard is inscribed: 'This Lionel Lukin was the first who built a life-boat, and was the original inventor of that principal of safety by which many lives and property have been preserved from shipwreck.' Lukin tested his first 'unimmergible' boat at Ramsgate in 1785, but the boat was later confiscated and burnt by the authorities because it was being used by local smugglers.

4. The Enchantress Tower is one of the Martello Towers built along the coast to defend against Napoleonic forces. It stands on the west bank of the River Rother in Rye harbour, at the entrance to Frenchman's Beach Holiday Park. It is known as 'the Enchantress Tower' after HMS 'Enchantress', a sloop that was beached nearby in the 19th century and used as a watch house by the Sussex Coast Blockade.

5. Her Majesty Queen Elizabeth, the Queen Mother, who served as Lord Warden from 1978 until her death in 2002.

6. Faversham was the birthplace and main centre of Britain's explosives industry from the 16th century until 1934, when its explosives works were closed and production was transferred to Scotland – it was foreseen that war might soon break out with Germany, and Faversham was too vulnerable to air attacks or invasion. Faversham's first gunpowder manufactory was the Home Works, established around 1560 and rebuilt in 1759. The Home Works included the 18th-century Chart Gunpowder Mills that still stand off Stonebridge Way, where the three key ingredients of saltpetre, sulphur and charcoal were mixed and incorporated together to become an explosive mixture. Chart Gunpowder Mills are open to the public as the oldest surviving gunpowder mills in the world; gunpowder made there was used by Lord Nelson's fighting ships at the Battle of Trafalgar in 1805, and the Duke of Wellington's army at the Battle of Waterloo in 1815.

7. Samuel Plimsoll was the originator of the Plimsoll Line which marks the safe loading level on ships; if the line cannot be seen, it indicates the ship is sitting too low in the water and is thus dangerously overloaded and in danger of sinking. The Plimsoll Line has potentially saved the lives of many mariners.

8. 'Owling' was the smuggling of wool out of the country to the Continent, in defiance of a protectionist law forbidding the export of wool to safeguard the English textile industry from foreign competitors.

9. The Channel Tunnel runs from Cheriton, near Folkestone, to Sangatte in France. The spoil excavated from the tunnel during its construction between 1988 and 1998 was transferred to a site on the coast between Dover and Folkestone, where it forms a chalk cliff coastline called Samphire Hoe. This is now a nature reserve where many rare chalk plants grow, which attract a wealth of butterflies and other insects.

10. One of the round objects set into the church tower is a cannonball which was fired at the town from a Dutch ship offshore during the Anglo-Dutch hostilities of the 17th century, hit the church and embedded itself into the stonework; the other round object is made of stone and was added to the tower many years later, in the cause of symmetry!

FRANCIS FRITH

PIONEER VICTORIAN PHOTOGRAPHER

Francis Frith, founder of the world-famous photographic archive, was a complex and multi-talented man. A devout Quaker and a highly successful Victorian businessman, he was philosophical by nature and pioneering in outlook. By 1855 he had already established a wholesale grocery business in Liverpool, and sold it for the astonishing sum of £200,000, which is the equivalent today of over £15,000,000. Now in his thirties, and captivated by the new science of photography, Frith set out on a series of pioneering journeys up the Nile and to the Near East.

INTRIGUE AND EXPLORATION

He was the first photographer to venture beyond the sixth cataract of the Nile. Africa was still the mysterious 'Dark Continent', and Stanley and Livingstone's historic meeting was a decade into the future. The conditions for picture taking confound belief. He laboured for hours in his wicker dark-room in the sweltering heat of the desert, while the volatile chemicals fizzed dangerously in their trays. Back in London he exhibited his photographs and was 'rapturously cheered' by members of the Royal Society. His reputation as a photographer was made overnight.

VENTURE OF A LIFE-TIME

By the 1870s the railways had threaded their way across the country, and Bank Holidays and half-day Saturdays had been made obligatory by Act of Parliament. All of a sudden the working man and his family were able to enjoy days out, take holidays, and see a little more of the world.

With typical business acumen, Francis Frith foresaw that these new tourists would enjoy having souvenirs to commemorate their days out. For the next thirty years he travelled the country by train and by pony and trap, producing fine photographs of seaside resorts and beauty spots that were keenly bought by millions of Victorians. These prints were painstakingly pasted into family albums and pored over during the dark nights of winter, rekindling precious memories of summer excursions. Frith's studio was soon supplying retail shops all over the country, and by 1890 F Frith & Co had become the greatest specialist photographic publishing company in the world, with over 2,000 sales outlets, and pioneered the picture postcard.

FRANCIS FRITH'S LEGACY

Francis Frith had died in 1898 at his villa in Cannes, his great project still growing. By 1970 the archive he created contained over a third of a million pictures showing 7,000 British towns and villages.

Frith's legacy to us today is of immense significance and value, for the magnificent archive of evocative photographs he created provides a unique record of change in the cities, towns and villages throughout Britain over a century and more. Frith and his fellow studio photographers revisited locations many times down the years to update their views, compiling for us an enthralling and colourful pageant of British life and character.

We are fortunate that Frith was dedicated to recording the minutiae of everyday life. For it is this sheer wealth of visual data, the painstaking chronicle of changes in dress, transport, street layouts, buildings, housing and landscape that captivates us so much today, offering us a powerful link with the past and with the lives of our ancestors.

Computers have now made it possible for Frith's many thousands of images to be accessed almost instantly. The archive offers every one of us an opportunity to examine the places where we and our families have lived and worked down the years. Its images, depicting our shared past, are now bringing pleasure and enlightenment to millions around the world a century and more after his death.

For further information visit: www.francisfrith.com

INTERIOR DECORATION

Frith's photographs can be seen framed and as giant wall murals in thousands of pubs, restaurants, hotels, banks, retail stores and other public buildings throughout Britain. These provide interesting and attractive décor, generating strong local interest and acting as a powerful reminder of gentler days in our increasingly busy and frenetic world.

FRITH PRODUCTS

All Frith photographs are available as prints and posters in a variety of different sizes and styles. In the UK we also offer a range of other gift and stationery products illustrated with Frith photographs, although many of these are not available for delivery outside the UK – see our web site for more information on the products available for delivery in your country.

THE INTERNET

Over 100,000 photographs of Britain can be viewed and purchased on the Frith web site. The web site also includes memories and reminiscences contributed by our customers, who have personal knowledge of localities and of the people and properties depicted in Frith photographs. If you wish to learn more about a specific town or village you may find these reminiscences fascinating to browse. Why not add your own comments if you think they would be of interest to others? See **www.francisfrith.com**

PLEASE HELP US BRING FRITH'S PHOTOGRAPHS TO LIFE

Our authors do their best to recount the history of the places they write about. They give insights into how particular towns and villages developed, they describe the architecture of streets and buildings, and they discuss the lives of famous people who lived there. But however knowledgeable our authors are, the story they tell is necessarily incomplete.

Frith's photographs are so much more than plain historical documents. They are living proofs of the flow of human life down the generations. They show real people at real moments in history; and each of those people is the son or daughter of someone, the brother or sister, aunt or uncle, grandfather or grandmother of someone else. All of them lived, worked and played in the streets depicted in Frith's photographs.

We would be grateful if you would give us your insights into the places shown in our photographs: the streets and buildings, the shops, businesses and industries. Post your memories of life in those streets on the Frith website: what it was like growing up there, who ran the local shop and what shopping was like years ago; if your workplace is shown tell us about your working day and what the building is used for now. Read other visitors' memories and reconnect with your shared local history and heritage. With your help more and more Frith photographs can be brought to life, and vital memories preserved for posterity, and for the benefit of historians in the future.

Wherever possible, we will try to include some of your comments in future editions of our books. Moreover, if you spot errors in dates, titles or other facts, please let us know, because our archive records are not always completely accurate—they rely on 140 years of human endeavour and hand-compiled records. You can email us using the contact form on the website.

Thank you!

For further information, trade, or author enquiries
please contact us at the address below:

**The Francis Frith Collection, Oakley Business Park,
Wylye Road, Dinton, Wiltshire SP3 5EU.**
Tel: +44 (0)1722 716 376 Fax: +44 (0)1722 716 881
e-mail: sales@francisfrith.co.uk **www.francisfrith.com**